N

CHOSEN POEMS

Songs and Ballads

of the Susquehanna

By FREDERIC BRUSH

INTRODUCTION BY

ARTHUR HERMAN WILSON

and

RUSSELL WIEDER GILBERT

SUSQUEHANNA UNIVERSITY PRESS

SELINSGROVE, PENNSYLVANIA

1953

811
B83c

28700
Ap' 53

Copyrighted 1953

SUSQUEHANNA UNIVERSITY PRESS

SELINSGROVE, PA.

Library of Congress Catalog Card Number: 53-7698

CONTENTS

INTRODUCTION

Throughout his life, Dr. Frederic Brush has been constant in his fealty to the Susquehanna country, all the way from Susquehanna County (his birthplace) near the Great Bend to the southern reaches of the river as it sweeps its way to the bay after hundreds of miles through the heart land of Pennsylvania.

In prose as well as in poetry, Dr. Brush has captured much of the rugged strength and grandeur of spirit to be found not only in the great valley itself but also in its people, with whom he most closely associates himself. Three books of poetry and two of prose have preceded the present volume and have drawn their subject from the Susquehanna.

The Alleghenians is a book-length narrative poem, epic in character, telling a story of the Northern Tier in Civil War days and built around the large personality of Thirlo Bard. *Hillman,* a book of narrative poems, is likewise constructed mainly around Thirlo Bard. *Crooked River,* meaning the Susquehanna, contains lyric as well as narrative poems, portraying the life of the pioneer hill people. *Seven Round A Mountain* is a collection of fifteen up-country stories, mainly for boys. *Walk The Long Years* is a book of prose that includes widely varied pictures of men and places throughout the Susquehanna Valley. Its greatness lies in the richness of life which it portrays and in the firmness of its philosophy.

The present volume of *Chosen Poems* was made up by Dr. Brush himself, in the sense that he made his own selection of poems. The editors have been most willing to assent to his choice because they feel that he is the leading Pennsylvania poet of the present century in the field of ballads and songs.

Last year we asked the poet in a letter how he came to be interested in writing and what influences had affected his ideas, his reading, and his composition. When he answered, he had no idea that his letter would speak for him in print. Neither did we. But here it is.

"How I came to write? Mostly through the early love

of hearing and reading clear musical language, and my will. Influences? At seven to ten years, I was reading Charles A. Dana (a master) in the N. Y. *Sun*—editorials and all. At twelve, a complete Shakespeare, that old Goodrich 'History of the World,' and the Bible. At thirteen, Tennyson, Burns, and Poe—then Emerson, Carlyle, Montaigne, and Parkman.

"Very meager formal education. The back hill associates had limited vocabularies but said things 'to the point' (mostly silent). My father was a scientist, inventor, and great talker. Men came from afar to hear him. For years he took the 'Scientific American' (a language influence).

"No valuable preachers, teachers, or lecturers came our way. But for years of youth there was constant singing (good quality) around the melodeon, with visitors from New England and our West—more cultured.

"Then not much formative reading or talk till in Boston (tired, and at medicine). I read widely the classics and all the best books—on street cars and walking and into nights. . . . In Hillman *Sayings* are my best word usages—and originality."

For those who grow weary with the daily tasks of life, the poet of Pennsylvania bears a refreshing song in his heart. Through him thoughts become music—not unlike the German romantic Tieck, who wrote: "Love thinks in sweetened tones." The poetry of Frederic Brush is an entire symphony of words, exquisitely tinged with Pennsylvania soil and soul. His artistic touch harmonizes romantic longing and keenly observed reality. Unlike Tieck, he lives and longs with those he knows.

Reader, you too can feel the vibrating strings in "the Hamlet of Ineradicable Music":

> I have enjoyed songs, river flow,
> Children's eyes, the thudding blow,
> Spring water, smells, a hickory chair,
> The subtle willingness of air.

ARTHUR HERMAN WILSON
and
RUSSELL WIEDER GILBERT

Selinsgrove, Pa., 1953.

CHOSEN POEMS

RIVER

Flowing, falling, ever calling,
   Day and night and into day;
Born of ages' storms and rages,
   I shall see the world grow gray.

Flowing, flowing, ever growing,
   Downward to the sea I glide,
Fed by fountains from the mountains
   Where the cool mist-maidens hide.

All this throbbing, murmuring, sobbing,
   Is my spirit-stir in sleep,
And these bubbles all are troubles
   Cast up from the secret deep.

From the highlands galleon islands
   Sail forever toward the south,
Bowers clinging, gay birds ringing,
   Never fearing flame or drouth.

Anxious lovers to my covers
   Come for troth and ageless dream,
And their sighing, bearing, dying
   Merge with the unfaltering stream.

Falling, flowing, never knowing
   Turn to doubt nor time to pray,
I am giving to the living
   Of my being, all the way.

Mara in the sounding gorge
   Heard the waters sith and fall
Down the old flume's mossy length
   To the ruined wall;
Heard the spray-fog drip and drip
   From the mouldering undersill,
Till with evening shadows came
   The Spirit of the Mill:

   "Mara waiting, Mara won.
   So life's stream doth run and run.
   Give—love and give, nor count each cost,
   For love is never wholly lost."

Mara sat very still
   And felt her heart's blood pause and flow;
It was as if a hundred years
   There did come and go.
Mara clutched the laurel stems,
   And tried to know what she had heard,
Straining to catch from out the mist
   Again the whispered word:

   "Mara waiting, Mara won" . . .

She was too young to hear and know,
   Too old to laugh and go away,
And so she sat beside the mill
   And listened every day;
Leaning by the glossy flume
   Where the waters glide and fall,
Heard once more from out the mist
   The wandering Spirit call:

   "Mara wondering, Mara won.
   So the stream of life doth run.
   Love—give and love, nor count the cost,
   For love is never wholly lost.

With You

I will go with you as the rose of dawn
Upon the forehead of the bolden day;
Bring the wild love that bears me from the home—
   Adrift, away.

I will be with you all the sullen noon,
Sore where you bruise, and gladsome in your pride;
Hold the worn love that queries nor repines,
   To eventide.

I will fare with you on the craggy hill,
Where headwinds beat or bitter demons lour,
Until we see the beckoning hand—and know
   The crowning hour.

I will lead with you down the sunken road,
Unto the river, in the waning light;
Wait the old love that trembles through the dark
   Of the last night.

Sudden Is Beauty

Sudden is Beauty.
We ride, climb, sail for it, wrinkle and peer,
Through chaffer and wine, quote, scribble, shun duty;
Turn the head—it is here!

Never long.
Face it, every pore open, quivering neurons bare;
Sway momently, strive, cross with banter or song—
Only trees and a river there:

'Tis a woman sewing in half-light, blue of a shawl,
Wild horses, the back of a worker, minute of storm
      that is fear,
Shades in a coffin pall;
Then star eyes and away—Beauty the antlered deer.

FIRE AND SON

Fire
Eager, dire—
Eons ago met life, sticky, penumbrous, dull;
Then a cramping, indrawn tendril of pain
There in the steam and rain
And the slime of immanent soul.
And a speeding of carnage and change,
By a few million years—
Till somewhere a smile, and tears,
And desire.

A son!
Immortality begun—
Of a kind.
Mind
May run
Beyond death:
Sung breath,
Poem, war, smile,
Hot hand or word,
Quiver awhile
Through heart and aching scar,
Near—afar,
Fainter—unheard.

But he
Is spirit and bone,
Cell of our cell
To reduplicate, swell
Doing and look;
Iron, wood, lime,
Out of love's burning,
Earth grown,
To earth returning
All he took.
We inhabit—we are.
No swirled mist of a star,
Nor a sigh

Wind blown.
Son,
A small victory won
Over Time.

DROWNED

I have no shame that I sang through the rift
And laughing leapt among them on the bar,
Not sorrow for my soul's too early scar
As there withdrew youth's gift
    Of utter hopefulness—a sobered year
    From seeing one so lone with many near.

She quivered down as with an ague chill.
A whimsy smile lurked on the boy's wan face
Turned full into the sun. We curved a space
About them and were still.
    Ripe summer droned with life in flower and tree;
    From the cove near a thrush sang cruelly.

They brought the little clothes and spread them on.
One kneeling murmured: "He was loaned awhile,
And now is taken to the Master's smile—
A heavenly embryon.
    Pray, and rise." With tortured look and hand
    The mother drove her back into the sand.

"We are whirled midges in a storm," I said.
"Old Nature gleans and moulds and random sows,
Rears beauty on decay, annuls our woes,
And recreates the dead.
    And you shall rest in Her, and soothing time."
    She crumpled lower in the river slime.

Then one drew off an eager babe from breast,
And wound her warm arms round the shaken one:
"Weep, Myra, weep with me for your lost son,
The hour is not for rest."
    They broke and made a litter of my oar—
    And passed with shining faces up the shore.

CONOWINGO

I met a girl in Conowingo,
   Footing up river when I was strong;
Wherever I've gone walking after
    She has been along.

There was beauty—but I remember
   Only the smell of evening's cool
And one gnarled gum tree holding over
    Flame above the pool.

Maybe it was her true upstanding,
   And level candor of life-desire
In eyes that held below the laughter
    A flicker of hooded fire.

So we go reeling once up-valley,
   Earth-enamoured, hard of thigh,
Singing into the dark and thunder
    Of echoing gorge and sky.

Years run like the lower river—
   Sun-reach, riffle and boulder-spray,
With hidden coves of scummed slack water
    Lingering in decay.

But some things are that don't grow older,
   Dreams may rival the worth of truth,
Ever the Conowingo maiden
    Stands in a glowing youth;

Beckoning often where night lours
   And stony up-roads slime with rain,
Ardor after second fallings
    To go on again.

Hours from the haze of old Octobers,
   Some generous greetings as we roam,
Faith of a friend and love's pressed roses
    Are all we carry home.

HEMLOCK

Hemlock, tell:
"I am of strength and beauty.
My sawn beams stand
Upright in silent duty.
My lifeblood clothes the feet of men;
They come and crowd and pass—and then,
Sometimes I list to hear again
The echoing warrior yell."

Time—mopes
Beneath your brooding cover.
In layered rings
The storied centuries hover.
You stood when yeomen left the shore
To stem the rivers, breed our lore,
Where scions of the seed you bore
Climb the cool north slopes.

Cleave, bind
With hidden tendril fingers
The sliding soil
While on the rock it lingers.
Lord of Pennsylvania trees
Proud of the eagle, glad of bees,
No poison for a Socrates,
Nor jealousy of kind.

Give—all!
There's a time to yield and gather.
Home builders call;
Go naked to the tether
Of singing chain and barbed steel,
The ripping spud, the iron heel,
To merge—and raise the common weal
Higher by your fall.

DUNCANNON

As I was walking through Duncannon
   (Go on if love lies dead)
Her voice came over, leaded, broken—
Fairly I knew what had been spoken—
   "After four years," she said.

Then heavy the road below Duncannon.
   ("Four years"—and the dark)
I saw in leafy, shadowing places
Those two unmasked, averted faces,
   Motionless and stark.

An old moon sank in gap Duncannon.
   (Cheer, or walk away)
Red life is here for its own faring,
Bounden to front, alone, unsparing,
   Another chancing day.

Bright rivers wed above Duncannon.
   (Dead love may guerdon be)
And many a twain since I went walking
Have stood beside that path low talking,
   In doom or ecstasy.

I have strolled far from dim Duncannon,
   (Bared faces and the years)
With yellow summered miles and seeing—
To know the memorial gift to being
   Of even love that sears.

FROM YOU LIKE A STAR

I do not love you for love's bliss alone,
   The ardent hand, or murmured pledge retold,
Nor night's rose kiss full-blown—
   Though these gone, we are old.

I love you for the things unsaid, the sphere
    Of tenuous effulgence raying far
Beyond the homely year
    Out from you like a star.

And backward to that hour of clouded sun
    You cleared by faith and longing, and were still—
As rounder life we won
    There on the thorny hill.

And though the road be upward yet, the crest
    Go by unknown, we shall see in the gloam
Your colors flare the west,
    Our lovebirds winging home.

HANDS

Hand—
A creeping fire
Of wonderment, desire,
Soft fingers, breeze of south,
Rain over drouth;
For who these and whispering lips
May withstand?

Hands
That hover and wait,
Press, dissemble, and mate,
Timing, telling as no words may
Pride of a day;
Curious, having more ways and weapons
Than love demands.

Tendril hands
Of infants, and the old,
In good-bye clinging, cold;
While round hard tools mid-age
Keeps heritage:
They love and nurse, they war and pray—
All time, all lands.

Song Of The Hunted

Awake, awake, the sun-kiss take!
  And blink the rheumy eye,
Lead freely in the open,
  Let out the wild woods cry!
    He came to snare,
He came to kill—
He of the iron arm and will,
But under the cliff he lieth still—
  And no one saw him die.

Breast and cleave the frosty air!
  Beat the blue lakes to foam.
Tell all the young in nest and lair
  The highland yet is home.
    He came to kill,
He came to snare—
But the gray fox found him lying there,
And dark red was his matted hair—
  Roam, ye of the forest, roam!

Then awake, awake, and the sun-kiss take!
  We have turned the evil thing.
No beast shall drag the red leg home,
  No bird the broken wing.
    He came to maim,
He came to kill—
He of the iron arm and will,
But under the cliff he lieth still—
  And no one saw him die.

Lorena Through The Frosted Pane

In Mountain Valley morning comes upon the gray
    moon-glow
When all the gorges lie in fog and dreaminess below.
    There days are long,
    Worn memories throng,
    And longings overflow.

Lorena through the frosted pane of her brown cottage hold
Looked out on tinted snow ascud o'er miles of dreary
      wold.
    The wan sun stole
    Into her soul,
    For she was growing old.

Strange phantoms whirled: her soldier love waved from
      a distant rise;
Is that her girlhood self that veers along the gale and
      cries?
    Hand-vow wed, the child
    Still-born, by leaves o'erpiled—
    Forgotten voices, eyes.

Some creature of the whited road, seen full two hours
      before,
Had won the slopes and lingered now a mile below her
      door;
    On the uptrail
    In dire travail
    It fell to stir no more.

Upthrough the drift and shriveling cold, bound on the
      wooden sled,
By superwoman dole and stress, were he alive or dead,
    In mother thought
    The man was brought
    Unto her narrow bed.

Lorena bared the traveler's face and gazed into the eyes
Of youth's lone love come wandering back, as homing
      night-bird flies.
    Long she knelt
    And quivering felt
    The withered past arise.

In Mountain Valley love strikes down like summer noon
      cyclone,
All sure delights of yesterday so fleetly to unthrone.

Pent hates flame,
Till shrived and lame
Hill prisoners lie alone.

When the old maiden's tears had passed as wanes the
      showered stream,
She rose with widened querying eyes and cheeks'
      unwonted gleam,
    To dower there
    With wondrous care
    The salvage of a dream.

Years of prisoned womanhood enwrapped the frail
      outcast.
At dawn he smiled, and knew her face and babbled of the
      past.
    It heartened so
    She did not know
    That life was ebbing fast . . .

The hearth-smoke died; till neighbors came and wondered
      to behold
One sitting by a stranger corpse in misery and cold.
    "The man is dead,"
    Was all she said,
    "And I am old—am old."

THE STRINGS OF LORIE

Loren, Loren, we have come to hear it.
    Take it from the high hook and rosum up the bow.
We're all the way from Growetown, seven miles or near
      it—
    And a long way to go.

He only pressed the baccy down, looking sad and steady
    Way across the Blue Ridge to a tired sun.
Music will come pouring when the heart is ready
    And the tinglings run.

How he held and fondled it—baby-like and tender.
　　Slowly on his dun face a rosy color grew.
Never a fiddle-neck so queerly curved and slender,
　　　　A bow so true.

Over on the hillside a sleepy bird went singing,
　　Somewhere in the night grove a morning sparrow
　　　　　　trilled.
Crickets murmured in the grass, the bells of heaven were
　　　　ringing,
　　　　All the valley filled—

Filled and bent to the waves of Lorie's playing,
　　Rolled from cliff and forest-bank to the river town.
Out upon the young dark startled life came gaying,
　　　　The hills leaned down.

Now he is bowing it elbow-high and limber,
　　Toe time-tapping and fingers on the run,
Maple fiddle calls to the sugar-maple timber
　　　　And they weave one.

Lift of the dance, the old jig tunes tirling,
　　Leaves and the little people all in the reel,
We and the moon and the tree-tops whirling
　　　　To the hornpipe squeal.

Then with cheek upon the viol, eyes unwinking,
　　The music fell and whispered in the songs of years,
Love and the moors and a storm sun sinking—
　　　　Memory and tears.

　　　　　　·　　·　　·　　·

Loren, we have been and heard—the road lies yonder:
　　But we are not the same men that came across the hill.
You have made us child-wayed, listening, and fonder,
　　　　Loather to kill.

And tomorrow in the hard field, and many morrows after,
　　We shall hear you tuning with the wind in the leaf;
Dance and death and heart-break, wondering and
　　　　laughter—
　　　　A balm of grief.

TSEN-MIN

"The Mummy of a Little Girl"
(Metropolitan Museum of Art, New York)

Why do I think of you here in the eddying Susquehanna,
  little Tsen-Min?
My canoe swerves and returns, and the current of life
Streams around me in loving and strife;
All lose and all win.
The leaping fish bends swiftly downward under the law
To death in a larger maw.
Infinite destinies in the ooze my gentle boat-waves shift.
Swallows are gleaning numberless perfect lives in the air;
The osprey over the rift,
And the spider poised at the mouth of his cruel tenuous
  lair,
Strike and feed and are stricken in turn, as I circling
  drift—
  And dream of you, Tsen-Min.

Many years have I gone to you there in the gloaming
  corner, silent Tsen-Min.
All day the sober querying people leisurely pass
Your straight swathed form in the glass.
Once as I stayed late in the shadow aside,
A high-blooded Saxon school-girl came and stood at your
  feet,
And quietly cried.
Then knowing the hour if ever was come, bending low
I called, for a whispered olden word, or sigh,
Or even a moment's glow
In the gathering dark of your dusk-brown orient eye, and
  your smile—
  As once by the Nile.

No answer; yet I will go to you, sure of our lives
  intertwining unto the end.
If you are silent there is to be no calling out of the past.
Only life-waves last:

Trembling on through myriad other circles of love and of
    will,
To break at eon's end on a distant shore,
Lulled in the final tapering roar;
Merging at intervals in a passing life with doubled power,
The lowering urn of being to refill—
    As you in me this hour.

THE PERFECT DAY

The Hermit of Elk Mountain used to say:
One perfect day
    Comes in September, fused of earth and sky,
    Wherein to sink and lie.

And cure the stammering that through a year
Of brag and fear
    Shuttled beneath our bravest word and smile
    And crazy-quilt of guile.

Then itching worms are numb, no insect stings,
Nor lover oversings.
    Lay all you are close to the cousin ground,
    And hear earth's axle sound.

No plan and no desire nor bound nor noon;
A rind of moon
    Nicks the west hill, the sun is all about.
    Red infires are gone out.

Somewhere far off a chipmunk stays to rhyme
Forgotten time.
    The slender tinge of blood-ripe in the leaf
    Revives no ancient grief.

Lay to the mold; the cares of being seem
Inept as dream,
    When for a spell the locomotive will
    Visions and is still.

WYOMING BROTHERS

"_____ *Cook*
_____ *Cook*
_____ *Cook*"

(Wyoming Battle Monument)

Three young men
Dead on a plain
By a bright river.
Owning no land,
Dreading no law
Nor fate nor man—
Why did they plan
To die so soon,
With friendly sun
On the hills as ever,
    That afternoon?

Not nameless then;
Somewhere a mother
Dowered them well.
And when the red fiends
Poured from the marsh
With finishing yell
Steadily on—
Maybe once again
Brother called brother,
    "So long, John!"

A step away
In the forest marge,
Love, work and years
Beckoning lay.
But they had quaffed
America's streams,
Seen the embers
Of Liberty fires,
Caught rare gleams,
In the clear light

Of fairer dawns
And the eagle's flight;
So in that hour
Could do no other
Than on Freedom's flame
Throw life and all—
    Even name.

SINNEMAHONING

How we sang at Sinnemahoning.
    Joan, Wissie and River Lon,
Youth in a glamour bending over
    The frail melodeon.

Sang and dreamed by the Sinnemahoning.
    Bull-toned Lonnie and alto Wis,
And clear through all, the fluting of Joan
    Warm as a stolen kiss.

Rosin the Beau, Eau Claire, Lorena—
    Dulcimer twang to the Lushbaugh Girls,
Young Charlotte of the lonely mountain,
    And Luliana's curls.

In the Black Forest snow went hissing.
    We threw the beech logs on the fire;
And from the toils of olden lovers
    Drew vision and desire . . .

Now Wissie lives by the great west water.
    Woodman Lonnie is far at sea.
And Joan here by the valley window
    Will come and sing to me—

Something true from Sinnemahoning;
    Winsome Kitty of Coleraine,
Pinery Boy, Bright Alfarata—
    Till we are young again.

Boy Lost

Wilkes-Barre, in the high oaken railroad waiting-room
A crowd curves upon a darkened corner
With a fringe of the moving curious
Peering through or over and going dubious ways.
"What's your name?" cooed the woman in black,
  Kneeling by a small, two-garmented boy on the bench.
"Dave"; and again he answered only, "Dave."
A policeman appears,
  And the lad's eye brightens a little as man to man,
But with puckered mouth and cross-eyed, level stare
He settles closer unto himself and will say no more.
A held smile crinkles the officer's lower face—
Knowing better than weepy women or mothers
The devious ways of youth.

"Lost boy—ragged and lost—a poor boy!
  Here's a banana. Bring a tumbler of milk.
Is anyone doing something? A doctor here?
Oh, the poor mother at home—"
Alone in a triple circle of alien eyes,
Wet hair and clinging shirt,
Night and a windy rain.

But we saw you well, little fellow—
Set of your neck and brain between the ears,
Straight back and blue-tight hands to the settle's edge.
Davie, Davie—you are not lost! You are found!—by life,
And the earth and luck and the farthest stars,
Law and courage and love—and the rim of the ultimate
      dream.
Morning rebellion, venturer's primal urge,
Out of a night's mysterious growthy change,
Drove you into the streets, and never again
Will you be baby-mine.

Lost? If any, we are the lost,
We of the gaping crescent round, in our tangle of
      harried hours,

Boomerang thoughts, forefendings, tortuous safety
    grooves,
Tissue and spirit hardenings and the drive of herded
    getters-on.
And we would go with you, laddie, to refind
The wonder round the turn, intimate rain,
Morning-glories on the wood-house wall,
Creek water in the ears, dire warnings, friendly mud—
To drive the bleared horizon daily back,
And turn the stone that bothered yesterday
And is outgrown to-morrow.

Found! in the station at Wilkes-Barre—
A boy named Dave.

MARBLE AND BRONZE

Look on the faces
Of them that last
Out of all past,
Climes and races—
Burthened and ghast,
Scored as with fire,
Dearth and desire;
Life's chosen band,
Grimly they stand,
Marble and bronze,
In the open places.

Toil or brief splendor—
Choose ye, and hold.
Love to the bold,
Grace for the tender.
Girding all here
Is that slow will
Urging us still
Through aging and fear,
Earth and heart's cold,
To endless endeavor;
Never surrender.

UNADILLA WOMAN

Singing in the morning,
On a hillside where the land is stony,
Through fog and rain
A ballad of old lovers
Comes down broken
With sounds of moiling and the cry of children—
One in illness.

How do I know
Eyes were hazel-brown and flecked
With fire-points, and her bosom
Ample for all homing heads,
Sweet breath and song-words?
Drifting below the island screen
No oar broke my harkening—
Till the airy cadence faltered, died
In purr of waters.

Long day down
Through hidden hills and mellow steaming pastures,
By sewer-mouths of towns, droll fishermen
And swart teamsters at the ferries cursing—
I bore her voice along,
As a friend's call out of absence, wondering
How much was her very own, or whether
Harmony would come to others—me,
On gray mornings, living so
By the river.

Woman is the river,
Threading ripple-song and mirrored heaven
Through the human jungle;
Draining wood cave bog, absorbing, fining
Slime-water, rain and soil—
Merging all, yet all alone;
Never pure but purer
Ever by a ray, one fine hair-breadth of measure,
Than the river border.

O the crooning mothers!
And smiling ones that hover others' children;
Rose-white, ebon, brown
Arms through murky ages holding
Tender life or weary.
Wherever love infolds,
And roofs are thrown over age or mewling,
And men go silently
To toil or foreign legion there will be
Unadilla woman
Singing in the morning.

SEVENTEEN

Karen by the gateway stones
Felt the blown cloth shape her bones,
Every bone and hollow rife
With coming beauteous woman life.
The wind went through, the wind went round
With a cooing woman sound;
She knew the night's desire to shower
Brooding love, a sky-borne dower.

Karen in the pond at eve
Let the hill-wine buoy and cleave.
"I ride, I stay, the water goes,
  My health is like a morning rose."
Leaf dusk bowered she heard the day
End moiling in the near highway:
"Shall my pearl body know the grime
Of road and mill—the ash of time?"

By twos the beaver swam, the snake
Went questing in a silver wake.
Kingfisher passed with loaded bill,
Karen only floated still:
"If all the living love and strike,
  Why should Karen prove unlike?
When comes the masked arranger's call,
I will say, Here!—I will give all."

LOVE WILL GO OVER

"Don't cross tonight!
Come to the door.
In through the roar
Hear! do you hear
The bicker and snarl?
(Was that a scream?—
Choked at the close)
Your father in dying
Held to one fear,
Of lost river-men crying,
When the loose timber runs
On June rising water.
Merriman's daughter
And the pink neighbor girl
Will grow fonder, more fair
For some waiting and dreams.
How it blackens out there!
Can a river have anger?
I am your mother,
Don't go tonight."

Far in the morning
Came knocking her door
Old Binney the raftsman,
Quietly saying,
"An hour or more
I am hearing the call—
First it came clearer.
Drowned river-men crying
Mean someone is dying
Alone on the uplands,
Untended—or nearer.
Where are your boys?"

From their unruffled cots
To the water she ran
Calling each village man.
Waiting long by the edge

In a lull of the rain
They heard a thin wail
From the Mad Devils' Ledge—
And again.
"If their father were here
He would bring them to me.
Is it drowsing or fear?
Do our river-men fail?"
And for manhood's token
They laid one son,
Gasping and broken
On the sand by her feet
In the morning. . . .

"Love will go over.
Maids not to blame,
I was the same.
Man is the rover."
So she lay dying
Many years after.
June rising water
Roared on the ledges!
"I hear you crying,
My river-men bold!
Here is your daughter—
Lover—mother.
Love will go over!

DEATH AND THE OLD NURSE

Two nights in the big house parlor they sat up with the
    corpse.
The low talk wandered through tangled hit-and-miss
    lives, foretellings, southern prisons, haunts, the
    never-seen-again;
His fights and wrastles and how he heartened the sick,
    of widows leaping in graves and married two
    months after.
Till Alzira Griggs the old nurse—who had served three
    generations and seen two doctors tire and pass—

Grew voluble as the rain beat under doors, and the tea
    and cider-brandy sissed in the ears;
Telling slowly, as one come from an alien journey, and
    drawing others' musings—of dyings and the
    foredoomed:—

Fannie Odell in the room with seven mirrors and pale
    green shades
Had us change her all to pink, and rosebuds pinned,
And the damask lamp-shade tilted so,
When every move was smothering agony,
"My color; draw the other curtain a trifle." That was the
    last she said.

Two parlors full of relations and some in the garden
Bothered Squire Allenby down with a second stroke,
And owning four places and cash, with never a will made.
"Do you want to say something now? Do you know me,
    uncle?
Is there anything on your mind that we can help settle
    or ease?"
So they came and whispered and went, with a thinning
    at chore-time.
Sundown he beckoned a neighbor and mumbled,
"Bring me a drink from the lower spring, go deep with the
    long-handled dipper."
He couldn't swallow by then, but buried lips and nostrils
Low in the cup, "Loren, that's the best water
Ever came out of the earth." And so ended.

All night Charlie Snedecker drove the team in the woods:
"Whoa, Sambo! Hi! come off that rock with your danged
    old muddle toe-in feet.
Steady, Jennie my girl! Now get your bellies low
For the mud-hole under the hill. Hang on, Sambo—
    hang!
Your wiffletree's going back.
Are you letting a woman pull the blue clay over your
    eyes?"
Eight in the morning he cleared and the minister came:

"You can repent and be saved yet, Snedecker, pray with
     me."
I never forget the long look Charlie gave, and motioned
     his son to come.
How well the dying sometimes speak—language like
     morning thinking, as it should be all the time.
"Take care of Ollie, Frank." (The one with whirling fits,
     you know.)
"Pipe the spring to the house. Let timber grow awhile.
  Pay the two notes—I have done as I have, and couldn't
     change anything much.
  You've been good to be with." He seemed to watch us
     awhile, with boring eyes—but wouldn't say any
     more.

I liked the way of J. R. Edgerton's quitting.
Ninety-one he claimed, but the Bible birth record got
     torn out by children playing cigars.
"Don't fuss around," said he, "everything's going smooth.
  I'm cold to above the waist and a wrinkle or two won't
     matter.
Go out and pitch quoits under the window, I can tell
Ringers and swatted hubbers by the sound. I've liked
     that sound,
And flails in the barn, and hoot-owls after midnight.
No more sniffling here. Be glad you saw a man
Live ninety years in rocks and average air.
Ah! under the heart now—easy—easy enough."

Elliott Beers in the war
Never got further south than Philadelphia,
Lived on relations mostly and liked to introduce
Independence Day speakers and talk of heroes,
Keeping read up way back of Mars and Napoleon.
"I want to die in action!" he often told,
"Facing odds—with a cry they shall remember."
  But it didn't come that way. Three of us got him out of
     the
  Mussy bed onto his favorite couch; but he called us
     ungentle,

And passed away whimpering for a change
To his old unscratchy nightgown.

Will Seaver hung on the gate in the cheery April sun,
Hollow-white with a two-year cough.
Clink of hammers came from the railroad quarry below,
"Do you hear them?—puddin'y sounds! There ain't no
      first-class strikers any more.
No one round here could sink a drill with me in my day;
Blue-stone, shale or bowlder—steadily down she bored.
Everything I had went into the whip of the *final inch*
      that counts, on any tool.
And I'll be back there showing them how again by June.
I feel strong this week!" He gripped and rattled the gate,
Then slowly his hands followed the pickets downward—
And we carried him into the house.

Everyone half pitied Mrs. Terwilliger,
Way back there, and he couldn't raise yellow turnips,
Nor get any children, and drowned in the creek coming
      home drunk from Tunkhannock.
I could generally see a reason for everything except
      cancer.
Pain, pain! and I've never felt bad about fooling young
      Doctor,
With doubled opium doses and all the paregoric
We could scrape in the neighborhood.
Worst was the waking, always waking to pain,
With a look of puzzle and horror for awhile.
And we were dumbfounded to hear her, that last hour,
Say: "I've had my share—a wonderful life,
With all the seasons and clever creatures and smells and
      berrying and reading and friendly women.
I would like to see things come out of the ground once
      more.
But I've had my share." That time I cried off and on
For two days after.

A Grain Of Sand Is Turned

When Uncle Elim died in our spare room
   I went outside to see
   Breezes in every tree
And through the night a tiger-lily bloom.

Two rams were thudding fiercely in the lane,
   A wood's-cat rubbed the door,
   The creek was in a roar,
Along the range the forest fired again.

While near within the shuttered parlor close,
   Odorous and ghast,
   Red-eyed women passed
With whisperings of old and coming woes.

I ran—and waded in the marsh's rim.
   The swamp life trilled and teemed,
   Bit, loved and fared, nor seemed
To worry at the shrunken plight of him.

Friend water-snake below the wooden bridge
   Tongue-dared, and dodged the stone.
   'Twas good to be less lone
And feel the silent stinging of the midge.

Came Elim's only son, stare-eyed and took
   A share of dulled amaze;
   Then wandered cousinways
To play together by the unfaltering brook.

Bees swarmed, the heifer freshened, oxen ran.
   That day the phoebe's nest
   Was builded to its crest
Above the window of the whitened man.

Not destitute the valley—Elim gone;
   Even so young we heard
   The gentle, earth-breathed word:
A grain of sand is turned, go on—go on.

GRAY WORLD

In dim side rooms, on bolstered cots, or rocking, rocking,
Old or young with the same python eyes,
Pale waiters, bandaged, crutched, drained lean,
Smiling at moments ease of pain—
These saw gray, and heard the axle turning:

The hue of the world is gray.
Splendor of young eyes,
Storm-bow, oriole, flower,
Blood's red and the rose,
Hill-framed lazulite skies
And the sun-path's gold—
Are fair guests of an hour;
Trembling they glide
From our too eager hold
  And shade away.

Mainly we come and go
In a sombre tone of mist,
Hovering night, wan spaces,
Rock and the endless slime,
Bearing over and through
(Like a color of thought or time)
Birth-cells and all dead faces
And those no longer kissed.
The rarest noon
Flaunting tinted graces
Over morning's rime
Wanes and merges soon
  Into afterglow.

Happier those who feel
Early in life's travail
The great winds hurrying by
Colorless or pale
With spindrift of the plain,
Long fog over seas,
And the infinite dun waste.
Less in vain
Shall seem the immuring haste

Of beauty's hour to these;
Undismayed and hale
Graciously they stand
   Deep in the real.

And joy the more when flare
Autumn, youth and star
Gayly athwart the west,
Signaling with deed,
Aureole dream, desire,
Love-illumined quest.
For the *Clearers answer with light!*
Glow in the woods, strike fire,
Press where demons lour,
Beam on the edge of night;
Never crying need
Of torch-boy, sunnier days,
   Nor a heaven afar.

MARSH CHILD'S LULLABY

Fair Colyn is going to sleep
Down where the throaty peepers peep.
Where brown waters dimly creep
Sweet Colyn is going to sleep.

There the pale-eyed pickerel lads
Doze beneath the lily pads;
And fifteen hundred frogs or so
Have no other place to go.

Within the old stump's hollow cup
All night the waves go plup-plup-plup.
And when the sky is clouded o'er
Sometimes you hear the hornpouts snore.

Hark, Colyn! Along the grass
I hear the whispering marsh-breeze pass.
It wanders off across the hill,
And now the very stars lie still.

LOST ISLAND

"Why the doleful Island name?"
　　She asked the river men,
As they went rafting gayly by.
　　A lover told her then:
"In memoried time, old Indians say,
　Twice it has grown and washed away."

Down river, dying fever burned—
　　"Too young!—Unfair!" she cried.
"Bury me on *Lost Island* prow,
　　Where through the yellow tide
The river men so lithe and brown
Every spring come singing down."

They buried her an April noon
　　Deep in the Island loam.
And did she hear the captain shout?
　　The oar-plash in the foam?
The squealing logs, the snub-rope whine?
And smell again the mountain pine?

A huge raft tore the guardian trees
　　And sheared the Island head,
The river gnawed the Island core
　　To gravel bars and sped
In a smooth planing, wide and free;
And she went faring to the sea.

Now when the night comes early down
　　And head winds rear the foam,
And the black ledges looming rend,
　　And raftsmen think of home,
Sometimes they hear from out the mist
A calling to the olden tryst;

A voice from underneath, ahead,
　　Or in the dismal air:
"I run below, I wait beyond,
　　And I will meet you there."
Then cold hands falter on the oar,
And all eyes seek the haven shore.

The Marked Man

Scorn grannies' mumbling if you will,
Rud Mirador was *marked with light,*
And dreaded lowery times and night,
From borning on June's longest day
Outdoors at noon (and talkers say,
Fathered on a shiny hill).

He climbed the peaks, lay naked out
In upper pastures (so the yarn),
Clave windows in the house and barn,
Drove back the forest edge too well,
And when the great trees roaring fell,
"Earth's love—the sky-kiss!" he would shout.

Once as he hammered at the wood
A traveling preacher bellowed in,
All hell-fire and original sin.
Rud stroked the trunks with even pace:
"Apparently in either place
The illumination will be good."

For living of a life too glare,
And thoughtlessness of those in gloom,
Death bent him to the black-hole tomb
All through a glistening day in spring.
"Maybe this evens everything,"
Was heard of neighbors gathered there.

They found him with the house aglow
In mid-forenoon, pine-torch and lamp—
"Dim, dim!" he said, "and strangely damp;
Clean the smutched globes and feed the log.
You fade like goblins in a fog.
How long before the dawn-up now?"

Toward evening in a smiling sun,
"What ails the light?" wailed Mirador.
"Out—to the hill!—I see no more!"
There on the wonted knoll he died,
With a lit lantern by his side—
A womb-marked man if ever one.

And wakening in the night, faintly far on
    mountains—
The hounds!—If a dog will cling three days
To a stretching thread, with belly glued to the spine,
We can get up in the morning, follow some quest,
Talking less of weather and joints, and bed
Without a soapstone. So the lean dogs of Hardhack,
Ever the best, rang bells to the prouder valley:

    Ouw—ouw—ah-a-r-ouw!
    Straight over the ridges now,
    North into night and snow,
    Through hills I do not know
    The Stoneboro big fox goes.
    Blood of my ears and tail
    Drops frozen on the trail.
    Between raw stinging toes
    Drive the stubble and stone.
    And the lessening slaver dries
    Till my worn voice whimpers and dies;
    Yet I seem to be not alone—
        And I cannot fail.

    Ouw-ah-ouw-ah-a-r!
    I follow near or far.
    For he led me wrongfully up
    His reek on a moistened wind,
    Slittered my ear and grinned,
    And I but a wambling pup;
    Worried me into the wet
    Playing along the shore,
    Till my mother came over the moor—
        And we never forget.

    Ah-ouw—ur-r—ouw-ouw!
    Through laurel thicket and slough
    And trick of the icy stream
    I hold him here in the nose,

Chief of our ancient foes.
Sometimes I stagger and dream
Of home in the shady clove,
And the brown bowl by the stove.
Then a curling loin-pain grips
The cry from stiffening lips,
Through the snow-lit forest wan
A scent comes down the breeze,
New power springs in the knees—
    And I go on.

THE LAMP

Our slow up-train got sided for a western war freight,
And stuck an hour there in the freezing drift.
A jungle sallowed arm-in-sling Lieutenant—
I aided on the way with an unhandy dressing—
Pressed eager eyes to the southside window.
Three others saw the lone light over river
On the white hill slope in the forest edge,
Two diverse men with a glowing kindly woman.
(I couldn't tell if she belonged to either)
She said: "Sick child, or a grandpa sinking in,
A woman tending, binding;
It's way past midnight, I can see it all.
I hope they have a good fire."
Then one man:
"May be a shindy—apples and hard cider
Stiffened with black-cherry juice and moonshine."
The other: "It winks, they're signaling the mountain—
Come for the deer spot-lighted out of season.
Or now's a time to touch-off Skinner's haybarn;
These hillions some are hellions."

Off at Callicoon the soldier saluting smiled them:
"The window lamp you saw there is for me,
Burning three nights—I got held by the blizzard—
Burning three years, maybe, I couldn't know.
I wish you love-lights at this journey's end."

Conover—fevered, or on splinted bone
Campaigning, honored, beaten, left alone,
Wracked and mortgaged by a wayward son,
Recouped by stone and wood, new-loved, undone;
Through all to dance and wrestle, and belong—
His coming, being, made a passing

Song for Middle Age:

Come in, swift years, and use me up!
By toil and sport and reeling blow,
Take youth's last drips of overflow,
Drain heart and head—and turn the cup.

The road behind is overlaid.
Here—is but hostel for a day.
All I have learned along the way
Is not to hate nor be afraid.

No more intent to scan the whole.
All things return; there is no haste.
The prayer is not to mire and waste
In some recession of the soul.

So on, till dimming eyes shall see
A moment in the wonted place
A fair hand, or a dead friend's face—
That fading turn to threnody.

Come, years! and tingeing brown to gray
Bring meed of peace, and share of pain.
Then let the hoary gatherer's wain
Find me beside the worn highway.

Auction

"Forty I hear—who'll make it the half?
Fifty—seventy—who says one?
They have rocked the same since love begun.
One-ten now for the maple crib.
Going—going!—that, young man,
Was the merriest bid you'll ever make,
For a babe's cry and a woman's laugh
Girdle the world and keep it true;
And all from a poorman's rib.
(Another is blushing somewhere here.)
Forty—one-forty—who'll cry two?
I see little ones' smile and wake;
Who knows the greatness of afteryear
This old cradle yet may hold?
One-forty—going, at forty—sold!"

(Neighbor)
Conover, being too soon born they say,
Lay there two years, doubting to live or die.
I wonder if Alzira Griggs was glad
To have him raised so—when all the valley seethed
Around his turmoiled years. Was the power
First bounden in that meager pint of cells,
Or did he garner from us, and the hills?
Coming this morning over Blue-berry,
Down the new-dug road where his will had way,
Sudden I felt great sorrow he was gone,
Who had fought me all a lifetime with strange joy,
Won land, rule, office, woman—well, you know.
Then it came: That all the people gathering here,
And others far away, had heartier lives
Because Alzira saved him in the crib.

"The yellow fiddle! Hand me the bow.
Ah, for a friend to stay so true!
I could draw the soul from it long ago,
When I beaued Marie on the Occanum.
Three is the offer—the half—make it four!

You buy no trinket of wood and glue,
But memory and the heart of song,
River bird warble and poet lore,
Throb of dance in midnight hum.
Only five for a famous violin
That has quavered you glee the valley long?
Six now—and a quarter—the half—say seven!
Who makes the spirit here within
May clutch a bit of heaven.
Bid joy till the last long bow is drawn!
Going at seven?—once—twice—gone."

On Monday morning of the day he died—
The old lady tells, and neighbors heard it too—
Myron got out and took the violin,
(His feet stone-cold, and trying hard for breath)
Smelled it and fondled every feature over;
And then with face aflush played slow three tunes—
Zip Coon, Doxology and Money Musk,
In tones that none had ever heard before.
First time I saw him in a harvest dance
At Tuscarora ere the mill burned down.
We quarreled and were parted by the girls—
How clearly I remember the two girls.
He had a lifting movement of the head;
And somehow we all knew a man had come.

"Hickory, dickory—'lo there, Doc!
Edge in close and back me up.
What's the mainest thing in life,
Lucre, wiving, health, or will?
Comrades and the cider-cup?
No, and here you buy it—Time!
Sing out, sing out! The day is thin,
And I am due in Luderville.
Half a dollar? Am I in
Nest of robbers? Hear that chime!
One now and for a cuckoo clock?
Running nimbly three lives through
(If this folded lovesick rhyme

Be left to prop the workings plumb)
Who shouts, who shouts? Go one—one-five!
('Tis stopped? Your dullness made it dream;
What's time if you are not alive?)
See! the wheels turn—this bird will scream
When hoarsening auctioneers are dumb,
And you all lie on Maple Hill.
Ten—twenty—thirty—going two!
And given away to Scrapper Jeem."

He never knew the inklings of a clock,
And measuring time by stints and chorings done,
Danced till the wick smoked, hunted coons to dawn,
And wouldn't leave the spearing till the pine
Fell through the jack and burned holes in the boat.
But she? We set fool watches by her call
Years in the valley, long and clear—"My-run-n-n!"
How solid all seemed then; no special end,
Just a slow dribble down, and sinking in.
Look round here! all I dread is, left alone.
Well, what's Luke yapping on these mutton heads?

"Who bids fair for the walnut bed?
Four-square standing the hundred year.
One dollar, sir?—no charity;
Generations foregathered here,
And there's honor if only in human life.
Borned and loving, tired and dead,
Tangled childer and new-brought wife
Gladly sunk to its whispered peace.
Two—and fifty—the quarter—three?
Hardly one curly panel's worth
To the opulent city artisan.
Bid up! for the commonest friend of man
All the old way from quivering birth
To welcome deep surcease.
Buy rest and kindness—sovereign cures.
Four-ninety—ninety and going—yours!"

When the big fire broke through in eighty-three,
The folks came down red-eyed with smoke and fear,
Until they sent for Myron Conover
At Traverton on Jury. Four wild days
He raged around the valley-head with arms
And scorched face swathed in dripping gunny-sacks.
When all was safe we brought him on some boughs
To this same bed; and now I seem to hear
The pitiable choking cry the woman gave.
I would not care to be an auctioneer,
Dealing with wreckage and the close of things.
Myron is gone; but I shall hold the dream
Of how he glowed in Tuscarora dance.
And called us leading there against the flame.

The Mounds of Men

Where are you, Myron Conover? We are here in the tansy
        bed by your cellar mound.
Myron, Myron! You must be somewhere about.
Your roses are out
Full, and another catbird quips and gurgles the same in
        the chokeberry hedge—
Ah!—you shivered me, woodchuck. All of your race
Stayed an eighty-rod circle away, in his day;
Nervy of you to breed under the front door ledge.
Clear the bramble and ground
From the bluestone upper step of the cellar stair,
Where the October cider barrel went down the slide.
How everything hurries to round
The angular turreted pridings of Myron—and hide
In a sullen quiet coating of lichen and tan
The work of a man.

We stumble over the earth on the mounds of men:
Temple, city and fort, mine, altar, beacon, road of old
        nations or fending wall—
They stiffen awhile to the gravity demon and then
Soften, fall. So far—and hold,

In a somber immutable beauty of line and slope,
Over the powdered bones, over the hope.
As the earliest man they are old.

Gone, all gone?—No?—man on before.
You are here! You are out on waves of all you bettered
    and bore,
Worthy progeny looking back this hour over seas,
Undestroyable heat of your ecstasies.
What if the thorn bush gains? Life remains.
Move on. Give another trial to trees.
Not years—centuries.
Root and burrow and frost
May cover and count you lost,
But this vined knoll ever will sign where you
With steady purpose and thew
Out of the muck and stony ground
Raised your mound.

FRIEND

As I stayed hopeless by the yellow mounds,
    Where all the garner of the bright years lay,
He came, and saying nothing did my work
    As 'twere a common day.

When the slow season turned, again he came
    And led me up where far the river gleamed,
Telling for hours of things that were to be
    Nobler than youth had dreamed.

Last shone the sun on our high mount alone;
    Olden truth in bannered flame unfurled:
The dark is rest, and ever sweeps the day
    Over a better world.

O Friend, you are the greatest gift. When fall
    The chill gray shadows on the path we roam
You come, and bring the love of each and all—
    Child, mother, brother, home.

POST-WAR PICNIC

The spiraling hawk saw, through the notches, up valley, over meads, down the ravines, by foot and wheel, even from the towns and city—the brightened people converging. Fair-weather picnic day in the country! If there be, out beyond hour-living and the end, heavens, ambrosial fields of pure content—here is one divination: they clasp, re-une, unwrinkle, laugh low, look longer in eyes, wives and husbands hardly know each other, old feuds go up in mist to the wondering birds. The hound years are back on their haunches. Time is inside.

Curved like a varicolored giant flower round the platform, they heard, patiently in hunger, prayer and spoutings and the gasping recitals of spindle-leg girls, till an older maiden sang in drooping tones,

Alone or Storm on the Bay:

> Golden sun in the piney west,
>   Ships of gold on an opaled sea,
> Ever go sailing and sailing by
> Into the night where the longings die—
>   And never come in to me.
>
> Silver moon high out in the east,
>   Silver ships on a shimmering sea
> Go sailing and sailing all trim and true,
> While I am waiting a word from you—
>   And never one comes to me.
>
> Lightnings cleave the glooming west,
>   Storm and night meet over the wave,
> And his ship out on that starless sea
> Is fighting for life and home and me—
>   Oh, if prayer could save! . . .
>
> Morn is streaming out of the east;
>   Blackest night and the storm's low moan
> Are over my soul for evermore.
> The neighbors gather about my door;
>   But I am alone—alone.

"And she too will be alone quite some time," said Wil-
cher Doolittle in a back row, "if my inculcations mean
anything. She's been drooling on that piece ever since
Stutter Osterhout shifted over to Allie McVey at Worfle's
huskin', and got married so quick he couldn't tell his
head from a dust-mote on a flea on the tip-end hair of the
tail of a mad dog. Everyone knows she's alone, without
chirping on it—and she needn't be if she hadn't read a
book once and got a lot o' misuninformation she calls
i-deels."

"That's a sad tune and story, though," ventured Bache-
lor Sill, "to be widowed with all your feelin's intact, and
no one to expatiate on."

"Wait'll you know a little more about widows—close
to," said Doolittle, grimly. . . .

Col. Thirlo laughed with a rocking head, and the last
curl-lip bitterness and rancor of war shed there—and
waifs of his scattered youth came settling home. He called
a young woodsman:—We have broken the walls of books
and are loose on the hills, with our own tooled mountain
words, our own poet!—you have heard of him? He weaves
the rhyme of his auger and ax-bit into the poem of here,
and goes hunting with music. Forester Reale! And the
tall youth, new-clothed, exotically handsome, dark-flushed
with thoughts of a mother and vision of Mara, drew and
read, from pieces of brown paper, a new ballad of

The Old Drunk Man:

> Too deep the ashes on the fire,
>   Too long alone with farm and wife.
> Pain, aging, stillness, love, desire,
>   Brown drouth of meadows and of life—
>   A little stammering of the will
>   And he is drunk in Luderville.
>
> Huddled, befouled, a stain of blood,
>   Inert as one that births or dies,
> From out the wreckage boldly gleamed
>   A mellow wisdom of the eyes.

And calloused worthy hands that gave
    Full story of the patient years,
Moulded by rock and tool and frost,
    The warmth of babes, the damp of tears.

Around him in the faltering day
    The village people pause and nod,
Under all the impartial earth
    At chemic play with king and clod.

Perchance the old man through the haze
    Was given a rift of vision clear,
And saw upon the encircled fronts
    Emblazoned telltales of the year.

And might have cried, "John Vellicore,
    A woman waits in Allentown,
Heavy and wan, to see your face—
    And when will you be going down?

"Jim Bourne, no tailored cloth may hide
    The poison cankering through your blood.
Yon bantering strong one stood and saw
    His friend go drowning by in flood.

"And you, young men, who laugh and leave
    To tell of this in church or hall,
Make honest livings forty years
    Before you judge of faith or fall."

O you, who turn the head and go
    Along the way with sober face,
(And if your gilded heaven be true)
    And come at last unto the place

Where all nations of the earth
    Their varicolored legions pour
Across that threshold of last hope—
    You may see through the narrowing door,
        All shining on the terraced hill
        The old drunk man of Luderville.

A hush, then a spreading murmur and growl as the Ludervillians drew together in knottings of pride-hurt indignation.

"Never mind them," said Thirl; "they will cool—and want fodder. Our picnic, this—and it's time they quit scoring hill people."

Mara Holden didn't like ruffles; whatever she wore seemed to say, I am the tonal cover of a woman. All in gold-vined green she stood by the organ. When only a little way in a song of Reale's to an old tune, through the crowd went whisperings, scornful faces and turning. Up sprang the Colonel and drew her to the very front, with an arm 'round quivering shoulders. There was silence. They saw the panther face of the soldier:

Neighbors, you have accepted me—for what worth; as you will Mara Holden, my ward, into your living and houses, when you have heard a story—that I thought never would need telling:

I lay in a creek-hole at Cedar Mountain, with blood spurting from a place I couldn't get at, and yipping for help. A Reb crawled around a rock and stopped it, with one hand—the other gripping his waist. "Where've you got it?" I asked. "In here," he said quite chipperly, "but I feel pretty good." We tried to yell together. Suddenly that look we knew too well came on his face. He was bleeding inside. "Yank," he whispered, "if you come through, get my daughter." He fumbled the breast pocket. "Take care of her—Mara—Mara." I found her in the west Maryland mountains, and brought her here.

Neighbors, I bow to you, all my life, for your mother-sister friending of this war orphan—who is not North or South, but the best of both. You would hang on the tail-ends of family-blood? I could tell you of her lineage, and have you kowtowing. But here she is, all courage, beauty, throb of life, truth. Not needing you—you need her!

RIVER MOUTH

So this is all. I thought to come
  Unstartled on the widening place;
  Nor feel this tingling of the face,
    And the core-fibres numb.

Yet something under earthly fear,
  Beyond all effort or dismay,
  Holds me unblinking in the gray
    Slow-eddying silence here.

Welcome a wraith, or lost fly's drone.
  Thanks now for all we don't foresee.
  I never dreamed that one could be
    So utterly alone.

Only it seems a waste of power,
  Augmented pain and crude satire,
  To have the heart-burn and desire
    Come unto this last hour.

When strength and virtues manifold,
  Mirth, fervor, beauty, courage—all
  So autumn kindly wane and fall,
    Where love grows illy old.

Clearer now it comes through this:
  These lingering things were ever best—
  Spendings, bold forays to the west,
    Mother and lover's kiss;

The armpit press of yellow flood,
  Tired farmers on a hill of flame,
  Strife unreluctant, furrowing shame,
    The taste of one's own blood.

Given the stream to cruise again?
  I would slow waters hurry through
  To play the rapids—fame or rue—
    With eager hearted men:

Of all the crowd along the way
  A crippled chore-man stays supreme,
  Who with true word and gay eye-gleam
    Memorialized a day.

Evening, near Roaring Spring
  Rowed two women lined and gray,
  Singing after labor's day,
    Laurel blooms to bring.

By Nescopeck (the night—how fair!)
  A Syrian maiden ran to me
  Crying half in fear and glee
    The fire-fly in her hair.

Through Mocanaqua in the gloom
  I heard youth and the dying sigh,
  The blow, the prayer, the birthing cry—
    As from a single room. . . .

Not memory these—each as a dart
  Of being from the darkening past—
  Life missiles, they come winging fast
    Into my stilling heart.

Where now the townsmen's reddening cheer,
  The medaled breast, piled gold and power?
  In this bald honest dying hour
    They are not here.

Nor largess well received and given,
  Sadness outdured, pains that rive;
  Only those meagre hours survive
    Were fullest loved or striven.

How many miles of smooth and rough,
  Hard-footed trails and spaded ground,
  With weary thinkings round and round—
    O, life was long enough!

No better chance by Helicon
    Or Tiber. Here was time, and hold,
    And all we stirred within the mould
    Inures and carries on. . . .

Gone are the querying and chill
    That trembled through an hour ago.
    Calm! One needs a death to know
    The turbulence of will.

My cells of husk are pale and thin
    This rapt engagement to appease;
    Yet, on the morrow even these
    New life may enter in.

Now memory, sea and sky are one,
    In them and darkness I am buoyed
    Mergent, resistless, undestroyed.
    How easily 'tis done.

LEAVES

April leaves—
    Like babies' hands enfold, uncurl.
    And we were boy and girl,
Where through long hills the wandering river cleaves.

Leaves of June—
    Wherein small myriad lovers mate and sing.
    We pledged with kiss and ring,
There on the steeps to carve our deathless rune.

Autumn gold—
    Mansioned, full-lived, resplendent, seeming wise,
    We paused and looked in eyes
One fulgent morn—and we were growing old.

Dead leaves—
    Beautifully we go down, and lie in peace.
    Not so to fail, nor cease.
Through things and lives our ample time inweaves.

FALL PLOWING

WHOA!—now I wonder where is the tip of that arrow.
Perfect twice—when it left the hand of the chipper,
And once again whinnying into the air
On its spiral way to the bone.
I hope whatever it was didn't struggle two ridges
To lie down here and rot. Twice perfect is something.
I've had once—when I first saw into this valley
And felt the man boil up and choke and the cloutings
Of youth slide off, and knew I had come to the place.
I'll hardly have it again though. I'll have hours.

Giddup! Whatever makes fall-plowing
So unlike any other?—ruminant, sad,
Sad-sweet like certain older funerals, weddings,
Frozen wild apples, low-throat singing of women—
Hasn't been told. You smell an essence of time,
Or a death-room closed for a season
And keep expecting to turn up money and jawbones.
Wild geese southing, children's voices farther,
Goodbye yauping crows and a feather of smoke
In air that breathes like liquor down to the boot-tops—
Somehow turns the mind outside of the skull-case
Ghosting mazily round over all creation;
I've fall-plowed all day and couldn't remember.

Once an Indian amulet fell off the moldboard,
Drilled, and smooth with a thousand years of fondling,
Of a rock they said was nowhere nearer than Canada.
New land here?—Only new men, blossoms and wood-
      chucks,
And nothing new in them but a feeling of newness.

Even the birds and horses know fall plowing
Isn't work, nor a purpose tearing into a hill;
Is a kind of dream, religious rite of a season,
Without a whip or gun, voices low—
To be done as well in spring if it weren't for the innards,
The autumn need of a truce and a scented delving
In the layered ages' wormy stubble and heartdust.

The Woman Who Came Down For Him

Going down from Baltimore
On the steamer Avalon
Seven men of everywhere
For the Eastern Shore;
One so knurled and illy wan,
Crumple featured, scant of hair,
Slued with palsy, cancer scarred—
Made it seem a trifle hard
For us to be jollying there,
Six brown huskies out of war
Marrowfatted, flush with prime,
Care o' women, scorn of time;
Brought a doubt if things were fair,
Where the jumble, whose the crime—
What such addled life was for?

Rocking through the Chesapeake,
Our doctor gave a steadying hand,
(Wondering if he had a voice,
Waiting for the squeak)
Felt we never more would whine,
Lighted him Sweet Caporal smoke,
Told of times when we were weak,
Queried where he hoped to land.
"Tyaskin on the Nanticoke,
God's own favorite basking place."
In the flare his smitten face
Glowed to sudden wistful charm.
"Never knew Tyaskin, Sir?
Come ashore tomorrow morn
Out to our new garden farm,
See the sun go through the pine,
And how thick the melons lie
By the edges of the corn,
Taste the sweet-potato pie—
And then watch the smile of her."

Morning we saw Captain Hurtt
Screw the sturdy Avalon
By the marshes nimbly through
A mile of thinnish dirt.
"Port Tyaskin!" some wag cried,
And rousingly the whistle blew.
I recall duck-hunters grim,
The buckled shed, a hound with fleas,
And two sad ancient cedar trees;
All's now dimming memory save
The woman who came down for him—
Of a brightness where she stood,
How both eager hands she gave,
Kissed with lingering look and hold,
Raised him queenly to her side—
Drove away into the wood.

"Skipper Hurtt, so gray and wise,
River people your worn book,
How gain and hold the glory look
We saw in her eyes?"
He mused the twisted channel through:
"Somehow in the underplan
Odd pairs ease the world along.
Women marry *round* a man,
Making things prove through him so
Often he is bound to go
Meandering in a pinkish fog.
Give *one* anchor holding true,
Eve's havening, and a snatch of song,
Fair aim, a noisy child or two—
There'll be homing in a bog,
Or the tinsel city crowd."
Mate says: "The Cap'n ought 'o know—
Being on his second cloud."

The Brim

I ran to the river brim,
   Crying—crying,
To lay all I held of him
By the rainy willow tree
Where a numb, seared half of me
   Seemed dying.

Morning I began to hear,
   Sliding—sliding,
Hill flood waters passing near.
Clouds flared with rose, bird-song renewed,
I felt the world's old plenitude
   Abiding.

So I arose and faced the sun,
   Reeling—reeling,
Into another course begun.
Following new dream and star,
Strong growths drew across the scar,
   Concealing.

Then out along the thoroughfare,
   Spending—spending,
Nerve and laughter, time and care;
And more I gave outright and gay
Came back threefold another day,
   Forefending.

Till from excess and new love's pride
   Glowing—glowing,
"Freedom, full noon—all's here!" I cried.
The old wound twinged, athwart the dark
A turning countenance passed stark
   And knowing—

Calling: Unbruised no life may run,
   Scaling—scaling.
Turmoil and joy are nearly one.
Wounds armor. Triers early know
'Tis in the plan to love and go
   Travailing.

All come to the river bank
            Weeping—weeping,
In wet weeds and forest dank
To lie through aging hours outdrawn
With no ease, no joy of dawn,
            Nor sleeping.

Some linger there, but they that rise,
            Braving—braving,
Have gleams of seership in their eyes;
The shaken ones they bind around
With strands of friendliness profound—
            Saving.

HARBOR LIGHT

Not all to raise a tower, an undying light
  Above the harbor gleam.
Will this dual flame illume the soul's grim night,
  The immuring dream?

America, too long you wait behind
  The shield of being young;
Recount your new bells cast, the charters signed
  Since Philadelphia rung.

Bend low and hear in clamorous aisles of stone
  Or on the prairies vast
Voices of legions still adrift, alone
  In eddies of the past.

Torch of Liberty, shine on—shine in!
  Through cellars of the mind
Until your beam on lord and manikin
  Anneals our humankind.

Where all may win the chance to veer and grow
  And press the bounds of knowledge and desire,
With imminence of mountain river flow,
  The eagerness of fire.

Squire Damon never laughed nor wed,
   Told a story, held a child.
   Grew the wonder why he smiled,
In the parlor lying dead.

Spoke an aged river man:
   "When the mobbing raftsmen came
   He beat them with an iron hame,
And chuckled softly as they ran.

"One time (it seems but yesternight)
   While new hill-people ran the town
   And all his projects voted down,
His countenance was ringed with light.

"They say a jealous, addled crone
   Cried sorrow on his childbirth bed;
   Others, a wild girl won and fled—
But so tis told of all the lone.

"Now who will salve our legal wounds,
   Bring the orphan in her dole,
   Keep our borough honor whole,
Run true line and set the bounds?"

Jamming ice or timber fire,
   How to marry, when to plow,
   Pestilence or broken vow—
Turned they to the silent Squire.

Rarely in his tired eyes,
   As they brought another load,
   Lava fires of humor glowed;
Then they thought, he grows unwise.

Living in the house alone,
   He could smell the deer at morn,
   Hear the growing of the corn,
And the river's undertone,

And the upper winds that tell
  Of the burning of the rain
  On the hills beyond the plain
And the shrinking of the well.

Doctor found his organs wrong,
  Tried more playful ways to teach,
  Drew the old Squire's longest speech:
"Each finds a crooked way along.

Where so many fume and guess
  Under screen of raucous glee,
  Going scared or giddily—
There is room for soberness."

Moulder of a stubborn race,
  Worn and grooved by mountain men,
  None could be so mean again,
Having looked upon his face.

Maybe that is why he smiled,
  Lying in the parlor dead.
  "He has laid him down," they said,
"Sweetly as a sleeping child."

PEACE

Morrows are of now
And the backward years that glimmer and run
Into mist where mud flats lay
And life crawled weakly out of the sea
To each eternity—
Then love and the wars, and "our day" begun.
Our day—of raining bombs, the gangster's silent
    cushiony ride to death,
Gas for infant breath,
Nations walled,
Hunger over the hill from rotting grain,
Stoned windows of the mill, dumb life
    burned and galled.

And yet—somehow, through the welter
    of told years, bemused, enthralled—
We gain.

Never as morning over the land,
Nor the trim legion band
Of victory. Our line
Is bent and tortured, as foam-front
    on the sand.
Forward here! the cry. This hour!
Storm the craggy chine
Of bigotry and grief and fisted power;
Up there—the sun!—
On, through the gagging choke—to dower
For everyone.
And while we shout, and rear the memorial stone
At spear-point of advance,
On either side in dire mischance
Our comrades stumble back beyond the trenches
    and the years-proud citadel;
Where the pale crosses tell
How they died.

If we believe the human race is young—
No bruised reptilia tapering into slime—
See, immured in forward time,
Nobler people, domes, religion,
Poems to be sung.
Peace? All life answers: only the more peace,
That fends and builds and grows
The sinews and the heart to weave or war again
With nature's endless throes.

If there be no way
To win the vaster kindness, banish fear,
Save through the near, the impending—gird
    and press
Some narrow salient outward where you stand,
Into the darkening and duress;
Nor wait the gathering of a mighty band.

Oh, yes—more light, machines,
Speed, leisure, loving, health, sons taller;
Grip the earth smaller, by air, undersea,
Crush ions, shoot the moon,
Change the zone, day and night cunningly:
These alone
Will never suage the jamming globe nor bind
Nations in fraternity.

The hope? In study of the mind:
Its breeding, molding
And neighborly unfolding,
By jungle-dark and fair degrees,
Through unimagined spheres.
No panacea, respite, charm that frees;
The hours of man are layered centuries.

DECADES

The past is dust of withered leaves.
　　Beyond—beyond? Ah, kiss.
All wealth and lore of ages lies
Here in the round depths of your eyes.
The proof, the potion and the prize
　　Are in the hour—and this . . .

Cold, my boy? The day is east!
　　Come, strive with me and know
The inner heat that mocks the sun;
We'll storm yon craggy mount and run!
And yet?—the grain-field to be won;
　　It lies there—and we go . . .

Then gently, as the bells are rung,
　　And questers gather home
With pensive eye, subdued of will,
Slowly above the river chill
The tired day spreads on brow and hill
　　Its healing monochrome.

HILLMAN

The winnowed sayings of hillman Bard,
By time and tongueing scoured hard,
Soldier, woodsman, farmer, sage,
Who went bold-eyed from youth to age,
Saw from his cove the same truths run
Through burg and kingdom, mote and sun;
And clement in life's waning part
Let the sure river lave his heart,
Content in time to pause and dream,
A gray-brown fisher by the stream.

In master trouble, toil or wreck,
Draw in the belt, and loose the neck,
    With blood in head and pouter breast
    Bear on; sheer luck controls the rest.

Second view of fact or word
Is better than the first or third.
    Deeds that morrows least rescind
    Are mostly done on second-wind.

When troubles flee, time lags, wealth pours,
Beaming friends hold open doors—
    Stiffen the ribs and spread the feet,
    Sudden side-winder blow to meet.

Ask not how far, nor of the storm.
Stride on, earth yields, an hour is warm
    Upon our road of glint and grime—
    Who promised any better time?

Success? To live a little higher
Than your friends and facts conspire.
    Cripple, president or fool
    Well are measured by this rule.

Work of morning's nervous rage
Least withstands the wear of age
   For every road and faith and right
   Someone toiled numbly into night.

See how the walker takes the hill
With lowered brow and stiffened will.
   He knows how many ills betide
   Untiming of the wonted stride.

Walkers learn through pain and rue,
'Tis foot must harden to the shoe.
   Blister-grooves with tough skin fill,
   Too many changes thin the will.

Everything passes. Know this young,
Your foot is on the second rung.
   When all ahead is dim with fear
   Say, "These will pass"—and crave a year.

Wind, rain, fire, surf, and the low seethe
Of brain at night, and all that breathe
   Vary one murmurous tone—maybe
   The core-sound of eternity.

"I love you!"—book and sermons close;
For once, one thing the groper knows,
   Sees from a center for an hour
   Pathway in a maze of power.

Spoke my boy upon the hill
Where our forebears lie so still:
   "If you must soon be buried here
   Why not play with me this year?"

Ready!—Now who will show my plan?
Calm. There is none, little man.
   Each day begins another year;
   Stars burn, earth heaves—and you are here.

The said word, like a sunken scar,
Holds on through death. How blest we are
    Along the later narrowing way
    For all the things we didn't say.

Defeat, wan cringing hours, jail,
Fire, fortune-loss, the gouger's tale—
    Well past; while still I inly groan
    At memory of a rude word thrown.

The best I own is what I owe.
One iron faithful rule I know:
    While I juggle, range and fife—
    Somehow I shall pay for life.

The river twines among the hills,
Quietly the new dam fills;
    Young straightener with the tensive nerves,
    Break, or learn the law of curves.

A stranger face gives all to me
Save the bone core of honesty.
    Read temper, travail, time and breed—
    Hidden lies the marrow greed.

Who will teach courage? Him we hail
The master; who by lonely trail,
    Chore and fear and thorny hill
    Firms the adolescent will.

The insect's tapered whing at noon
Bounds life—the old earth's major boon.
    "Hard luck?" You've had a trillionth chance
    From out the bewildering atoms' dance.

"Here was the poet's home!" They gaze,
And go earthwide divergent ways—
    Caring no more to read or quote,
    But simply that he lived and wrote.

I measure now this earthly span
By hours when I was my own man.
  We pass too soon from flame to gray,
  To quote and copy time away.

Not all to see and know and feel;
Tune in, beribbon, join the reel.
  The flower of life is fully blown
  To be seen and held and sown.

Aunt Emeline from early youth
Knew how to live with nearby truth,
  Alert to see each day unfurled
  Fresh ways of being on one world.

The sick are late; the river slips
Round them in a close ellipse,
  Purrs and soothes and packs the drift
  Where they linger on the rift.

Whatever woman yields at last
From dusk soul cellars of the past,
  Up through the salvage charred and dried,
  All of her loves rise glorified.

Immortal?—twisted, knurly Bard,
With all the in-man fiber scarred?
  And youth that wants this training ground,
  Without our shadows hanging round.

Through look and thinking, deed and child
We quiver onward, reconciled.
  And endlessly this body stuff
  Seeps into life and time . . . Enough!

Beyond the last imagined star
More awful times and spaces are;
  From this no-end all human press
  Curls back in stupored weariness.

What lingers? Youth's first stroke of power,
Three woods-fire friends, a mother's hour,
  Work that drove along new shores
  And lovers' greetings out of doors.

Work that spread beyond her door,
Two marriage ringings, children four,
  A sunken love-dream running through—
  The roundest woman life I knew.

Fairest mark for those that pass?
An earth-bank covered thick with grass.
  All they were and did and said
  Runs onto life's unceasing thread.

The happiest hour? It comes full-bloom,
About the bride, anear the tomb,
  With fame or void, in struggle ghast—
  Even it may be the last.

You seek the "haunted house"? Come in.
The ghosts of loves, the shades of sin,
  And wraiths of hope and smiles and care
  Creak nightly on this footworn stair.

My comrades mourn each cellar-mound,
Crying: "What use? All goes to ground!"
  But every home-scar signs a place
  Of service in the human race.

When you don't know what to do,
Wait and let the quiet through.
  Where y-roads halt your eager quest,
  Take one—it will seem the best.

Why live? I can not know—nor you.
He or It says: Shuffle through!
  With gift of life a sealed bond goes
  To will and wonder to the close.

Who scans the eras scarce may doubt
The race of man will taper out.
　Perchance to-day we crush or spurn
　The creature formed to rule in turn.—

But we are young, in racial teens.
Creed?—Enough, with simple means
　To have this youth mature and be
　Drawn nobler on eternity.

HALLOWAY'S BEE

Twenty men are forty-five, swaying altogether;
　Hay field, stony slope, gully road or trees.
Only dry-foot towny lads talk about the weather;
　And coffin-waiters brighten at the bees.

All that's done by nine o'clock goes to living longer,
　Dew and the morning fog save a lot of sweat.
Juices of a sunrise earth make you tall and stronger—
　But certain ones are never very wet.

Chime of the whet-stone over meadows calling,
　Birds and the women-folk pause and listen in;
Loud the four-wide cradle swish, breast high it is
　　　falling—
　And the lazy ones are where the grain is thin.

Fatty Worfle in a bog, seven standing over:
　It isn't him we're worryin', but how to save the boots.
Easing Wilch Doolittle onto bumble-bees in clover;
　Sticking boasted oxen on chained roots.

They were tired yesterday, and chary of their neighbor,
　But Halloway is broken down, his hook is in the beam.
Now the ax is finger-light, sickle is a saber,
　And proud is the lather on the team.

How can thirty little men swinging altogether
　Do the work of eighty and go laughing in the rain?
They have found elixir-land where trouble is a feather,
　And friendliness a fever in the vein.

The Mineral Man

The crazy mineral man goes by
With black divining rod on high.
He lives alone by Cobble Hill
And nary foot of soil does till.
And never when the farmers call
Will plant the spring or reap the fall;
Nor any gear or siller save,
Nor tote a neighbor to the grave.
    Gold and silver, silver, gold—
    The mineral man is never old.

All day upon the stormy hill
We hear the stroking of his will,
And pity the unreckoning cuss,
Full knowing how he pities us.
The jewel that he delves to spy
Is in his rapt and gleamy eye
That pierces rock and lures afar
And glitters like the red bull star.
    Gold and silver, lead and coal—
    The addled man is in his hole.

Neighbors' cattle in the corn,
Laddies crippled, maids forlorn,
Sugar charring in the pan—
Nothing turns the mineral man.
Rheumy morn or shut of day
Meet him striding miles away,
And see, when late with love we ride,
His lantern on some mountainside.
    Gold and silver, zinc or lead—
    Dig and hope till you are dead.

Yet when the seasons hale us round
To weed again the wonted ground,
Friendships wane and kissings cloy
And all our skills are little joy—
We envy him the fatal quest,

Burning sanction in the breast,
And sometimes wonder as we go
Who is high and who is low.
　　Silver, silver, gems or gold—
　　The mineral man is never old.

THE WALKER

Strong man stepping—what do you see?
　"Space, dun levels,
　　Ah, a spire—
　　So they crowd ever,
　　Pairing and fire;
An eagle curving this winey air,
Not playing, must be a river there—
　　And the timeless miles for me."

Stand awhile—look all around.
　"Tree circle, bronze
　　Sky line the same.
　　(Release, not giving
　　All things name).
Homes, and a feather of railway smoke;
No end while I smell fallow and oak,
　　And both feet spurn the ground."

Tablelands dip, you came a hill.
　"Why hold me here?
　　Hug your truths.
　　I'll keep love
　　(Better than youth's)
And venture, sinews rewound to ropes
From strings that quivered young fears and hopes—
　　Joy of hard-bitted will."

Nothing endless, some slopes are sheer,
　And room for falling.
　"You earned the yawn.
　　There plumbs the eagle!—"
And he was gone.

WHEN A MAN FALLS IN PRIME

I shall sing and dance,
Through variant ways and years however long.—
Sing now. Years have an organ-stop that tremors song.
But the sun is here, is time—and I have will.—
The time-sun pours and empties to refill.
And the ways have chance.

The pine is higher,
And idly knows how the chaffering millions fare
Underneath. Till a pungence grows on the air,
As a beautiful mushroom crayon cloud upheaves;
And deadlier at the great base piled with leaves
Strikes the fire.

Morning oriole flame,
Flutes of Maryland spring, on the ash's teetering spike;
A shadow, and from the hill—meteor of the shrike.
Verdant island below, playground, the otter's lair;
Burn and a gouging tide—now rapids glistening there
Have no name.

When a man falls in prime,
There's a moment's hush, and the few who are climbing
        or high
Stand, looking backward and fore with sobered eye.
The common close in, feeling largened, freer of breath,
More emergent, alive—when disaster and death
Ripple time.

Panic!—no ruling or norm;
Hurricanes tangled over a buckling earth:
We with war-face cleaving, tightened girth,
Pleaded, strove with the haggard, through city and
        town,
Bent, resurgent, buffeted, stripped—went down
Like an oak in storm.

If there's no faith in a rock,
How soon may a man go under his own debris;
Raising a battered head in the maze to see
The heel of a friend, cloud of a woman's face,
And all that owned him, triune love and the place,
To the auction block.

THREE STRIKES

Strike!—three.
Throw the heavy club away and wamble to the bench.
Time and tune and circumstance are screwing on the
      wrench.
  The world says, *thrice:*
  Three blind mice.
  This, that, tother.
  Wife, child, mother;
  I love you
  Rare stays two.

Three times—*out!*
Or—maybe in awhile, if the triune gods stand by;
For they like to watch the third kiss, foil or final try:
  Change, tax, death
  Sure as daily breath.
  Once, twice—sold!
 "Be bold, bold, bold";
  Three weeks or years
  Settle faith and tears.

Three swings—enough.
Curb the bitter lip-line and modulate the howl.
Siddown—the very first one might have been a foul.
  Trigons everywhere:
  Land, sea, air.
  Eat, drink, be merry,
  Briar, bloom, berry;
  So long, John!
  Going—going . . . gone.

Imperious as of yore
I hear your solemn roar
Come through the night-fog chill.
The town and woods are still;
Deep under nature's breast
  There is no rest.

With steadiness of doom,
'Neath ice, in summer heat,
You gnaw the indrawn feet
Of couchant Manatoom,
Till mountain and terrain
Are ground to like again,
Where levels of brown mud
  Allay your flood.

Here on the burial hill
Where elders watched us brave
In sport thy treacherous wave,
Above the cliff, sans will,
We gather stilly home
To merge in the yellow loam;
And wait till down your tide
In wheel of life again,
Harried by wind and rain,
  We too shall ride.

And far: through mother ooze,
Atomies' play, stressed rock,
Crystal, and earthquake shock,
Into cells that suffer and choose;
With ultimate quietness,
Or high on radiant wing,
In hour of heart's excess
  Loverly to sing.

All life feels, has soul,
Immortality—knows,

Timefully strives and goes
To death in the long parole.
Porch rose and crawling slime
Its quivering path in time,
Wind-tuning pine or snail
 Alike avail.

Your thund'rous voice shall die
On some last ebbing sigh,
And where stern tumult is
Brood the old silences . . .
Yet we go on awhile
Who held the crowded hill,
By spendings of love and will,
Stroke and valorous smile,
Deed and query and rime
Shed in passing time,
On tremulant life outborne;—
Perchance to see a plan
Somewhere through paths of man
 In the ages worn.

HAVING OVER

We think we would do otherwise—having it over.
 However?—
'Twas a plaster-cracking randy at Van Elsor's.
Ages back it seems sometimes; again I see and feel her,
Here as that sunshine on the floor—dark, rapt Elnora.
I was high-antler buck then, home from College, handy
With toe or casual girl. Soon after cakes, Elnora in the
 whirl
Made up to me, peculiar—times before she had been hard
 to reach—
And through till almost day I could sense her clinging,
With droop, hot hand and eyes—
Wide eyes strangely bloodshot through the gray.
Till I saw her man (they had been running two years
 close together)
Coddling a fire-haired beauty from the town. Then care-
 lessly I knew. . .

Noon, next day: "Wake up!—Elnora—
Nora Van Elsor—drowned in the lake!—You know Elnora.
Chore-boy found her early, all dressed for the party.
Only child— —only one. I go now to help. Come over
   for me."

The question—lifelong:
That night, if I had met her halfway, halfhearted even,
   playful rover—
Would she be grandma-dandling bairns—today?
It only takes a little, in right time, to turn a killing
   heartache tother way.
Maybe affection, any kind, degree, wherever, is to be
   grasped—unthinking.
There's one night I *would* change—having over.

White Water

At end of dreamy miles the curve,
   Roar, rock and stinging spume;
And what was life above, below
   May never quite resume.

The years no measure are; we go
   Dour on the holden way:
The mountain slips, fear thralls, love smites—
   And life pours in a day.

Give me the hours that overweigh
   Time, and rules of three;
Yielding torn visions through the mist
   Of an eternity.

The kiss that seals, death's honest face,
   The infant at the breast,
The blow, the hand-clasp and the tear
   Are more than all the rest.

FERRY

(At twenty)

> O-ver, o-ver, o-ver!
>> Ferryman, speed.
>> Link the new dream with deed.
> Out from the somber cove and tethering vines of
>> home,
> Down to the ships and crowd's good-natured, weav-
>> ing, narrow, gleaming ways, urgent I go,
> Over earth's last curve in the afterglow,
> Long and free to roam.
>> Ferryman, speed.

(Thirty)

> O-ver, o-ver, o-ver!
>> Ferryman, sing.
>> Bound by word and ring.
> Flower of the valley grown of sweetness out of our
>> hills,
> (Gently, ferryman) far she comes in joy to be
>> neighbor, lover, friend, and beauteous wife.
> Velvet the air inbreathes and the vale is rife
> With chime of a thousand rills.
>> Ferryman, sing.

(Forty)

> O-ver, o-ver, o-ver!
>> Ferryman, come.
>> Be as the river, dumb.
> It laved my moist red stains quietly dun and gray.
> A simple blow, but iron of the hame sank into his
>> head as he smilingly bore me down like a
>> serf or cur;
> We two there in the quivering hover of her—
> So sudden all's wreckage. Away!
>> Ferryman, come.

(Fifty)

    O-ver, o-ver, o-ver!
      Ferryman, row.
      What ails the river flow?
Bend, old man! We ride the race with death.
Her strange eyes drive me halfway wallowing here,
(Ferryman, press with the back—I have power, gold)
They were sunken fires, but her feet grew sweatily
      cold,
And the thing she would say came breath.
      Ferryman, row.

(Sixty)

    O-ver, o-ver, o-ver!
      Ferryman, rest.
      (Who knows which hour is blest?)
And watch the leaves going down gayly as ever they
      twirled
For we have had time, and a round of curious life all
      told—full gamut, from death to the dance;
Slid through a thousand bickering narrows of chance,
On the brim of a whirling world.
      Ferryman, rest.

      . . . .

(Eighty)

    O-ver, o-ver, o-ver!
      Ferryman, wait.
      Come early or come late,
      All the same to him now in the curly-walnut case.
The waters gurgle and purr by the river-road of his
      playtime and peace, and rare bold meteor-
      gleams;
But the wilding look, and the love and drive, and the
      dreams—
Are gone from his face.
      O-ver.

His Road

Young Heman built a road
"Where no road could or should be."
Hard liquor eased "Town Viewers" to unanimous acclaim.
They ran the line through ledge and bog: "Let him
    corduroy,
He likes work and woods, and women—and his way."
But Heme, who liked full loading on hard ground,
Grinned and curved it round.
The new route had a number, yet always bore his name.

Timber out, came fire and clearing meager farms.
Potatoes, butter, flagstone, berries, buckwheat honey,
    furs, hound-pups and moonshine stuff
Went down that rutty trail for money, just enough to
    stead
The backwash hillmen drifting out and in—till neigh-
    bors said:
"Worst ever happened here was Heman's road; handy
    awhile, and then
Brought on us low grade men, night rovers, starting fires
    and feuds—or an incidental child.
Their women, better—seem to make slow gains
Against grimed habit and men's blubbered brains.
Anyway, it's growing back to wild."

Long time after, in there hunting deer,
I asked a wandering ancient why the runway we were on
Went curling through the rocky forest like an engineer.
"Heman's road!" he said, as if I should have known.
On a log we smoked the breeze (against all hunters'
    rule).
He wanted talk: "I'm the last on it, living all alone.
Can just remember Heman's osier cane I craved. His
    last hike
Was here, found dead by roaming boys—on his own
    grading.

They told him he might come back horizontal,
Said he, 'I'm going to walk my road again.'
Not crazy, as some thought, only lopsided,
Not enough woman balance, too long roughing men.
City doctor came high-cost and breezy,
Was overheard to call it *e-gocentral.*
Whatever 'twas it didn't live with easy."

"What made him do this so?"
"They say he had to, Roman in him, always fevered when
    he saw a jungle,
Said a road marked longer than a temple,
Wanted sun let in, and plows and people.
And wasn't he righter than the ones who fought him?
Folks, most any sort, are more than deer and pine.
We may have been hard-looking, first come in, a little
    loose
On law and church religion; but someone must begin,
And toward the end our children taught the valley
    schools and married down the line.
Everything peters in a century—and should:
New ways and chances, hard knots, swamps, new girls
    and dances.—
See that gray fox loping?—Ss-t, don't kill.
He's coming Heman's road—as other thousands,
Four-foot and wingers, men and lovers will."

WINTER BROOK

Winter—and the music of the woods,
    Save some far-reaching cry
        From out the wildest deeps,
    Sinks suddenly into an icy sigh,
        And nature sleeps.

No whisper of the grass, the rivulet
    That all the summer long
        From underneath the hill
    Sent up unpraised a daily gift of song,
        Is hid and still.

Over the pallid slopes a silence broods,
  As unto death. Bend low,
    Harkening. Ah, there rings
  Through frosted forest-aisles a cadence slow,
    The brook still sings.

When winter comes upon my head and thine,
  With peace and childhood near,
    And hope in sunset skies,
  The few who bend and listen still may hear
    Faint melodies.

Epitaph

"His thinkings and achings are o'er"—
  On the native sandstone scrolled.
  Amply the tale is told;
No craving other or more.

Here lie child and wife,
  There his cellar scar.
  Some kindly achings are;
Thoughts, the flowers of life.

Over his field and mill
  Popple and willow grow;
  Back to the wild they go.
Enough of striving and will.

Far dim the Wilderness fray;
  On the brambled sunken grave
  Torn flag and roses wave,
Of some Memorial day.

Play and loving and sun,
  Unfruited sowing and fear.
  He came easily here;
Aching and thinking done.

BLUE JAY

Come soon and scream
In the dull valley here.
Shoot cerulean gleam
Through smoke and sooted glasses.
The tooled year passes;
Little to hold, regret,
Honor, acclaim—and yet,
Burrows the old unease,
For you in the orchard trees,
Aflash against the gold,
Jeerer, warner, scold—
Bantering away
     Time.

Jay, jay, jay!
Raucous, bright destroyer
Of quivering egg and young.
To you I am no toiler,
Only another crowder
A-reek of dogs and powder;
Who is right and wrong?—
You who know us better
Than you are known of sages.
And shall you go unsung?
Having been given ages
Of this precious sun-room?
Best is warmest, nighest,
Human at the highest
Has a cage and gun-room,
Feeds on lives—and rages,
     Between times the song.

"Man! Man!" you cry,
 From grove or wintry shock.
"Man there! Why, why?"
 And half around the world
 We bipeds queer have stirred
 As to a captain's word;

Straightened, made choice,
Felt will's rebirth,
Spoken, and wondered less,
Struck on through homesickness,
Found springs of mirth,
Scrawled signs, piled cairns—
And having surely heard,
Lone or with whimpering bairns,
On water, sand or rock
    Some flag unfurled.

BOBOLINKEN

Morning on the Beaverbrook I met a ribbon girl,
She made a kind of ready eye and twiddled on a curl.
No for me!—The *bobolinks were singing* all the way,
Rings and little *silver chains falling* in the hay.
    Bobolinken-unkum-inku-ting,
    Spinkle-spangle-ee-sulink-o-ling!
She was curious and playful but couldn't seem to see
I was kicking a tomato-can from home to Hickory. . . .

When I went down to see her, at seventeen or so,
With hair and shoes all shiny—she had another beau.
The bobolinks were reeling in a noisy mating spree;
They sang, Go back to mother and get on your dungaree.
    Bobolinken-unkum-inku-ting,
    Spinkle-spangle-ee-sulink-o-ling!
She grew high-chin and chilly—and I wished that I could
    be
Kicking on an empty can from her to Hickory.

The morning we were married my father drew aside
And said: "My son, you're starting on a memorabilious
    ride,
A far and foreign journey; I can give you no advice—
But our *bobolinks are singing* to your bird of paradise."
    Bobolinken-unkum-inku-ting,
    Spinkle-spangle-ee-sulink-o-ling!
She has been ever lovely, but one gladdest hour for me
Was kicking that tomato-can from home to Hickory.

Two Together

Stay, and watch the tired day sinking
  Below the hill where first we drew
That thin space nearer; I am thinking
  How your head to my shoulder—so,
    Comes ever new,
    Old as wooing
    Yet ever new.

In the close hours with you I wonder
  How any cause that nealed us one
Could gain by ending two asunder
  Who have outgoing joy and grace
    Only begun,
    Valor of living
    But well begun.

For there's other in mating than home and childer,
  Loving is more than giving all—
Visions outproving, powers that bewilder,
  And above and onward, seeming near,
    The spirit call,
    Two together
    Hearing the call.

Till the bounty fails, and we dissever
  Body and soul in the cosmic play;
Yet our gladness and work are one forever
  Quivering through new lovers athrong
    The grooved highway—
    Two by two ever
    Down the old way.

Send Me With Beauty

Prone drunk with youth and noon of summer day,
  The sky drawn low through clover frame above,
A white cloud slowly spreads to filmiest gray
  And vanishes like morning dreams of love.

Gazing into the blue unfathomable,
    Infinite, tomb of longings—I would know
In this brief bodying of the beautiful
    Is all, now wholly lost to all below:

The pliant spheres reune at some far height
    To sail the heaven in more resplendent form,
Flared by the dawn to warn the lingering night,
    Or arched with glory in the passing storm.

Old Beauty in and out with love or wrath,
    Dance-wreathing space and sun and lowly eye,
Flames in the alley, blocks the mountain path,
    Weaves on through life and death—and cannot die.

O God or force or mother or dumb cause,
    That brings us ever to an alien day,
If there may be no certitude nor pause—
    Send me with Beauty on the unknown way.

BEARDED MEN

The bearded mountain men came down
    To see the President.
Through modeled sentences and sound
Of law and casuistry—they found
        What he meant.

Slow eye-balled, quiet-handed, lean,
    Their feet enjoyed the ground;
They stood upon the city walk
And boys and drummers, goods and talk
        Went around.

But playing children hid behind
    Their booted legs, and then
Looked laughing up; and women gray
Passed dude and priest to ask the way
        Of these men.

The eye that is the torch of life
  Shone bolder in the face.
The nose leaped out, the brow was rayed.
About each visitor there played
    A space.

O bearded sires of early days!
  From camp fire, mart or sod;
The beaten, fearsome mouth-lines seemed
O'ercome, age terrorless—you gleamed
    A little more of god. . . .

The hairy men came down the roads
  To see the President.
"He is full set of brain and beard."
They garnered what he had, and cheered,
    And went.

MOTHER

With death at morn, a mild elation spread
  Through all the place; she had been ill so long.
    Her funeral day passed with strange energy,
      Brave word and song.

Kindness flowed from far unwonted holds.
  The hills drew near; fair gold the river shone.
    Only the father with an awful face
      Sat still alone.

Years ran and laughed with years. The wolf-pack cares
  Fled every morning from the front of youth;
    Joy in the hour, fear, wrestle, blood, and love—
      The clinch of truth.

Then from a height I saw the ends of life;
  A woman's footmark traced my thoroughfare.
    Turning to view the path into the west—
      She waited there.

Mother of men, forgotten of our prime,
  Silent beside us all the upward way,
    Lead o'er the plain to where the dun sky soothes
      The narrowing day.

To meet no more—hand, brooding look or kiss?
　　Some heaven then to know how far through me
　　　Flow measured streams of that primeval love—
　　　　An immortality.

And when the dark that is nor night nor shade
　　Steals down the casement, as the birth-light came,
　　　Like men before I shall behold one face,
　　　　And breathe the name.

SMOKE

Smoke of the maple grove.
The sap is up!—in the wood and the reddened girl.
Roar away, bluffer March, you may whiten, swirl,
But the syrup is somehow sweeter this year—and the
　　　kiss,
Where bubbles plop and the flame-caught drippings hiss,
In panther cove.

Smoke of the fallow-burn,
Billowing black, over the hills, cloud-high.
He has joined a wife, and signed it on the sky!
Struck—for the flowered porch, barn-swallows, grain,
Hard to the variant seasons, prize of pain—
And will not turn.

Smoke of the autumn leaves,
Breathed the world round, ages, ever the same,
Primal perfume out of lowly flame,
Till memory of the mellow fruitage of years
With falling leaves of the heart and falling tears
Interweaves.

Smoke of the hunter's pipe,
Gray-blue spirals carry up to the beams
Houn' dog's querying gaze and the master's dreams;
Two sound unregretters, likers of earth,
Three-way livers—toil and questing and mirth—
Character-ripe.

Smoke of the chimney-head.
Forty years across (did he mean to live alone?)
We timed our chores and noons by that signal cone
Rising slow on the mountain, neighborly, true.
"Furman has no smoke," said the boy—and we knew
He was dead.

WHY DO I LOVE HIM?

Why do I love him?
Tell the wind yonder
Stroking the river
To beauty aquiver
Never to wander
From the cool hill,
Rose not to spill
Heart fragrance, fire
Shrink from the tinder—
How can love ponder?
Destiny higher?—
I am behoven,
Mergent, inwoven,
Through—not above him.

All to come after?
Fair and storm-broken
Days of our living—
Spurn the misgiving.
He may go weary,
Slacken and lour
Under the years?
So I've had wooing,
Shared glowing and tears,
In scorn of undoing,
Grace will endear me,
If only I hear then
Clamor of children
Running in laughter.

A Song For Middle Age

Come in, swift years, and use me up!
  By toil and sport and reeling blow.
  Take youth's last drips of overflow;
Drain heart and head—and turn the cup.

The road behind is overlaid.
  Here—is but hostel for a day.
  All I have learned along the way
Is not to hate nor be afraid.

No more intent to scan the whole.
  All things return; there is no haste.
  The prayer is not to mire and waste
In some recession of the soul.

So on; till dimming eyes shall see
  A moment in the wonted place
  A fair hand, or a dead friend's face—
That fading turn to threnody.

Come, years! and tingeing brown to gray
  Bring meed of peace and share of pain.
  Then let the hoary gatherer's wain
Find me beside the worn highway.